D0583364

الـــواحـــــة للتأجيـر

OASIS LEASING

With our compliments

ABU DHABI — LIFE & TIMES

ABU DHABI
LIFE & TIMES

Through the lens of Noor Ali Rashid

MOTIVATE
PUBLISHING

Published by Motivate Publishing
Dubai: PO Box 2331, Dubai, UAE
Tel: (04) 824060, Fax: (04) 824436
Abu Dhabi: PO Box 43072, Abu Dhabi, UAE
Tel: (02) 271666, Fax: (02) 271888
London: Macmillan House, 96 Kensington High Street,
London W8 4SG. Tel: (0171) 937 7733, Fax: (0171) 937 7293

Directors: Obaid Humaid Al Tayer, Ian Fairservice
Editors: Ian Fairservice, Catherine Demangeot, Kate John
Editorial Consultants: Bob Milne Home, Peter Hellyer

First published in 1996
Reprinted in 1997

© Noor Ali Rashid and Motivate Publishing 1996

All rights reserved. No part of this publication may be
reproduced in any material form (including photocopying
or storing in any medium by electronic means) without
the written permission of the copyright holder.
Applications for the copyright holder's written permission
to reproduce any part of this publication should be addressed
to the publishers. In accordance with the International
Copyright Act 1956 or the UAE Federal Copyright Law
No 40 of 1992, any person acting in contravention of
this copyright will be liable to criminal prosecution
and civil claims for damages.

ISBN: 1 86063 022 7

British Library Cataloguing-in-Publication Data.
A catalogue record for this book is
available from the British Library.

Printed by Emirates Printing Press, Dubai.

While every care has been taken to identify
the people and places featured in the photographs
of this book it is possible that readers may be able to
provide further information. The publishers would
be happy to consider such additional details
for inclusion in future editions.

CONTENTS

ABU DHABI – A DESERT ISLAND
BLESSED BY BOUNTIFUL SEAS

LARGEST AND WEALTHIEST of the seven component parts of the United Arab Emirates, Abu Dhabi has a history that stretches back many thousands of years. Excavations by foreign teams and by the Al Ain Department of Antiquities and Tourism and the Abu Dhabi Islands Archaeological Survey have identified sites that date back to the Late Stone Age and beyond, proving that, since time immemorial, its people have depended on the resources of the sea and of the desert and its oases to make a living. Skilled divers began to exploit the fine pearls of the Arabian Gulf at least as early as 4000 BC, while the ingenious invention of the underground water channel, or *falaj*, permitted agriculture to continue in the inland Al Ain Oasis even after the climate began to become more arid around 1000 BC.

While little is known of the inhabitants of Abu Dhabi in those distant times, the Arab ancestors of today's Abu Dhabians certainly began to arrive in the area from Yemen and central Arabia by the beginning of the Christian era, adapting their own traditions to the environment and surroundings they found. Although the discovery by the Abu Dhabi Islands Archaeological Survey of a pre-Islamic Nestorian monastery on the island of Sir Bani Yas shows that at least some of them became Christian, the arrival of Islam in the middle of the 7th century AD brought a new faith to the people which they adopted with alacrity. It has remained a cornerstone of their beliefs – and of their way of life – ever since.

The first trace of today's emirate of Abu Dhabi in history dates back to the 16th century AD, when a book published by a travelling court jeweller from Venice mentioned a list of islands in the southern Arabian Gulf. To one of them he gave the name 'Sirbeniast' or Sir Bani Yas, evidence that the Bani Yas confederation of tribes, led for the last 250 years by the family of President His Highness Sheikh Zayed bin Sultan Al Nahyan, must already have achieved a degree of prominence in the region.

The Bani Yas themselves first appeared in history in the early 17th century, when they are reported to have been involved in around 1633 in a major battle between the coast and Liwa with an advancing army from Oman. Historical records trace the origins of the Al Nahyan Rulers of what was to become the emirate back at least as far as the late 17th or early 18th century, to the reign of a somewhat misty figure named Nahyan. He was succeeded by a son, Isa, and by the middle of the century, his son, Dhiyab bin Isa, had become the Sheikh of the Bani Yas, with his main base in the Liwa oasis, deep in the desert.

To Sheikh Dhiyab goes the credit of establishing the present-day Abu Dhabi, said to have been founded in 1761. A tribal legend tells the tale of a party of hunters from Liwa who visited the coast, and saw the tracks of a gazelle leading out across the *sabkha* – salt flats. Following the trail, they found it had come to a narrow inlet of the sea, which it had then crossed, to an island just offshore. Their pursuit continued, and, following the tracks through a thick sea mist, they came upon the gazelle drinking at a spring. While the tale does not relate what happened to the gazelle, the discovery of water on an offshore island was of more importance. Returning to Liwa, the hunters reported their find to Sheikh Dhiyab. Recognising its significance, he ordered that a settlement be established on the island, which he named Abu Dhabi or Possession of the Gazelle (*dhabi* in Arabic).

The choice was fortunate. The Bani Yas and their allies the Manasir already controlled the Liwa oasis as well as western islands such as Dalma and Sir Bani Yas. Between Dalma and Abu Dhabi lay some of the greatest pearl oyster beds in the whole of the southern Gulf, and, with an Abu Dhabi base, Sheikh Dhiyab and his successors were able to benefit from the revenues of the pearling industry. To consolidate that base, his son, Sheikh Shakhbut, moved his headquarters to Abu

Dhabi in 1795, building a small fort that today survives, much enlarged, as the Al Husn Fort. Such was the foundation of the emirate, although today it is revenues from oil, rather than from pearls, that make Abu Dhabi's offshore waters of such enormous significance to the economy.

Over the course of the next century or so, Abu Dhabi grew to become the strongest power in south-eastern Arabia. Inland the Al Nahyan Sheikhs extended their influence to the oasis of Al Ain, where they formed an alliance with the Dhawahir tribe. Offshore, following the arrival of the British upon the scene at the beginning of the 19th century, the frequent skirmishes on the pearling banks that interrupted the emirate's main source of income were brought to a halt with the agreement on a permanent Treaty of Maritime Truce. From that treaty, the area became known as the Trucial Coast or the Trucial States, a name that survived until the formation of the UAE in 1971.

By the end of the 19th century, the island town of Abu Dhabi had more pearling boats than anywhere else on the coast. Ruled between 1855 and 1909 by Sheikh Zayed bin Khalifa, the grandson of Sheikh Shakhbut bin Dhiyab and the grandfather of President Sheikh Zayed, the emirate was a centre of power and, by the standards of the time, of wealth.

◆ ◆ ◆

A PEOPLE SHAPED
BY THE LAND

A lifetime's exposure to the desert sun is etched on the face of a palace guard.

Keen-eyed, khanjar'd and carrying the ubiquitous rifle this gentleman presents a typical desert portrait.

Previous pages: Bedouin and their mounts — camels were essential to the survival of man in the Arabian desert.

WHILST THESE DAYS it is mankind that shapes nature, in the past the people and their way of life were moulded by the land and the climate. And although there is evidence that climatic conditions were marginally less severe in prehistoric times, the southern Gulf has always demanded strength and endurance from its inhabitants.

Archaeologists have determined that there were established settlements in the region as much as 7,000 years ago. Even those living in relatively fertile and prosperous areas such as Al Ain (an important caravan station on the ancient trade routes between Oman and Yemen in the south and the civilisations of the Euphrates and Tigris valleys in the north) led a hardy, frugal existence, their diet consisting primarily of dates, locally grown grain and imported rice – although closer to the coast this would have been supplemented by fish.

Clothing was designed to suit the climate and, although there were regional variations in style, all included the *keffiyeh* (headcloth) providing efficient protection from the sun. It was also customary to carry weapons – often a rifle or the wickedly curved *khanjar* (dagger) with its intricately decorated handle and sheath.

The elders in Bedouin society are accorded great respect.

Although camels were used for long desert crossings, donkeys were the main beasts of burden inside the oases. In the background are barasti houses, built from palm-tree leaf-stems.

LIFE IN AL Ain and other settlements, before the discovery of oil, had remained much the same for centuries, the people relying on what little could be coaxed from the reluctant land. The date palms of the oasis were of great importance: their fruit is of high calorific value and, when boiled, keeps for several months; their stones were crushed for fodder or for a form of coffee; their trunks were used for building; their fibres made into baskets and bindings; and their leaf-stems used for constructing *barasti* houses – lightweight structures, the open-weave pattern permitting any passing breeze to cool the interior. Other buildings were constructed of mud brick, often around a central courtyard, an architectural style that is often still seen in modern domestic buildings.

The camel's large, broad-soled feet are ideally adapted for walking on sand. Able to survive for up to three weeks without water they provided the only reliable method of travelling across the desert.

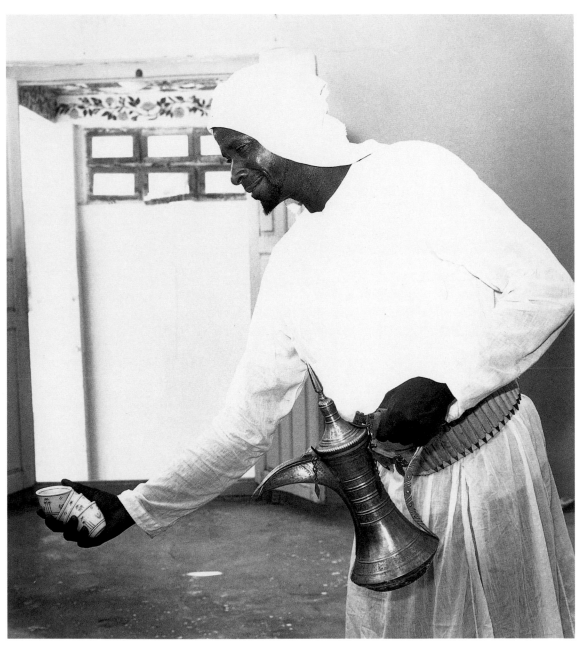

**Serving the refreshing cardamom-
flavoured coffee – a tradition
which happily still survives today.**

OUT OF THE harshness of the land – and the need for companionship, news and, often, assistance – grew the Arab tradition of hospitality. The custom of the desert demanded that travellers be treated as honoured guests with whom food and drink should be shared, welcomed by the phrase '*bayti baytak*' – in translation 'my house is your house'. Whilst the host was honour-bound to feed and protect his *dhaif* or guest, the Bedouin code was also practical – such shelter was strictly limited to a duration of three days.

The serving of coffee spiced with cardamom was, and remains today, an integral part of Gulf hospitality and the *dallah* – an ornately decorated brass coffee pot – was a prized family possession. The host would pour the coffee into small, handleless cups which would be frequently refilled. Polite guests would drink no more than three cups, indicating that they had had enough by returning the cup with a gentle shaking motion.

**Pottery, probably not dissimilar to
these jugs, has been made in the
Al Ain area for at least
5,000 years.**

A tobacco farmer samples his produce whilst waiting for a customer.

AL AIN LIES at the crossroads of two trade routes – one running along the edge of the jagged Hajar mountains from deep in Oman up to Ras Al Khaimah and the other leading from Abu Dhabi down Wadi Jizzi to the Omani coast at Sohar, at one time the largest port in the region. Al Ain was a centre for the sale of both local produce and imported items – from the Omani ports came coffee and cloth, rice and fish, pots and pans, as well as a variety of other staple goods.

Merchants and their customers traded mainly through barter as there was little currency in circulation. Where coins were used the Maria Theresa silver dollar dominated transactions in eastern Arabia until early this century when the Indian rupee was introduced. At this time a family, seeking respite from the humidity on the coast, could summer in Al Ain on as little as 50 rupees. By the mid-1960s the emirate of Abu Dhabi was using the Bahraini dinar as currency, which was in turn replaced by the dirham after the establishment of the United Arab Emirates.

Fair dealing – bullets and bottle balance the scales.

A falaj in Al Ain, typical of those which still provide water to the oases.

A trader and his customer discuss the merits of a water pot.

EVEN MORE IMPORTANT than Al Ain's location on the trade routes was the availability of fresh water. The *falaj* system is to Arabia what the aqueducts were to ancient Rome. In use at least 3,000 years ago – making the city probably the longest continuously occupied settlement in the UAE – the *falaj* taps underground supplies in the foothills of the mountains and carries the water through tunnels several kilometres long. Until as recently as the early 1970s the system was Al Ain's main source of water – it then supplied some 50 million litres a day – and gardens and date palm groves are still irrigated by the *falaj* system today.

The supply of water allowed the inhabitants of Al Ain to grow crops, including tobacco, dates and lemons, which they traded with tribesmen. It also enabled the community to support large herds of livestock, and to this day the city's camel market attracts buyers from all over the region.

In 1946 Sheikh Zayed bin Sultan Al Nahyan, the brother of the then ruler of Abu Dhabi, Sheikh Shakhbut, was appointed Ruler's Representative in the Eastern Region, based in Al Ain. The reforms he set in place included the building of a new *falaj* and the more equitable allocation of supplies to ensure that water became more generally available for agriculture. More importantly, he established a reputation for far-sightedness and shrewdness – qualities that would one day play a pivotal role in the establishment of the UAE.

Hard bargaining has always been a prerequisite of shopping in the souks.

Al Ain's camel market is still one
of the largest in the country.

This young cameleer takes a protective stance against the suspicious 'evil eye' of the imposing camera lens.

POSSESSED WITH ENORMOUS stamina, able to survive for long periods without water, and with the tough lining of its mouth permitting it to eat almost anything from thorn bushes to rubbish and bits of leather, the camel is perfectly adapted to survive in the desert. In addition to providing transport for men and goods and acting as a steed in times of war, the camel was valuable as a source of meat and milk, its dung was used as fuel, its wool employed to weave rugs and its skin to make water containers. Little wonder the Bedouin held the animal in such high regard. *Ata Allah* – the gift of God – they called it.

The first evidence of the domestication of the camel, dating back more than 4,000 years, comes from the island of Umm Al Nar near Abu Dhabi. Remains of the two-humped Bactrian camel have been found in archaeological excavations 50 kilometres north of Al Ain – although, sadly, none of these handsome beasts now roam the desert.

A camel caravan bringing produce from the interior to the souk in Al Ain.

Mutually refreshed, camels and
their keeper head out from a falaj
near Jebel Hafit.

TODAY THE TRIBESMEN of the UAE and Oman own some of the finest camels in Arabia – examples of which may be seen at Al Ain's thriving camel market which weekly attracts hundreds of buyers and sellers from an area covering many thousands of square kilometres and stretching deep into the Empty Quarter.

Whilst camel caravans, which used to travel as far as Jeddah and Damascus, no longer set out from Al Ain to cross the vastness of the deserts of the Arabian Peninsula, the beasts are still highly prized. Throughout the emirates the ancient sport of camel racing – originally just a way of testing the animals' speed, strength and stamina – is keenly followed, whether at the modern, purpose-built city racecourses or the less formal country tracks.

The Bedouin have always drawn great pride from owning fine camels.

Refuelling at a falaj near Al Ain.

IN THE 1960s the nine villages that made up the oasis of Al Ain – then better known as Buraimi – had a population of only a few thousand. Three of the villages, including Buraimi itself, belonged to Oman, whilst the other six – inhabited by the Dhawahir, the Na'im and later, significantly, the Bani Yas – owed fealty to Abu Dhabi. For centuries the complexities of the area had prompted the various inhabitants to build forts – leaving to the present day an intriguing architectural heritage. Most were built of mud brick on a stone base – leading one stiff upper-lipped Trucial Oman Scouts officer to comment that he didn't mind being attacked by cannon balls but most fervently hoped that it wouldn't rain.

Whilst mud may have had its disadvantages, the material was easy to work and allowed the builders to add decorative patterns, construct arches, shape crenellated walls and form latticework screens – attractive examples of which may be seen at Muwaiji – former home of Sheikh Zayed bin Sultan.

The oldest fort in Al Ain is Muraijib, built around 1830. Jahili, constructed about a century ago by Sheikh Zayed bin Khalifa, has recently been carefully restored.

Previous pages: Returning home with the groceries. This fort, Husn Sultan, with its square enclosures and round corner towers, is a fine example of a type common in the Al Ain region.

The stance of the sentry looks considerably more permanent and solid than the crumbling fortress in the background.

These two tribesmen sport the essential accessories – khanjars, rifles and well-stocked bandoleers.

A group of Bedouin on the edge of Al Ain regard Noor Ali's camera with varying degrees of suspicion.

THE INHABITANTS OF the Arabian Gulf have been renowned as warriors since their earliest history. The sword, spear, longbow and dagger were in general use from pre-Islamic times, supplemented in the mid-17th century by the matchlock musket. But in the late 19th century it was the .45-calibre Martini Henry rifle that was most commonly and keenly adopted. This simple, sturdy weapon was standard issue to the British Army and – despite its heavy bullet and vicious kick – it was accurate up to some 400 metres or so. The people of the southern Gulf adapted the original version, usually removing the protective wooden stock from the barrel and decorating the weapon with silver. Such was the demand for this popular rifle that the Royal Ordnance factories – in an early example of arms marketing – produced a special version for the Gulf, naming it the Martini Muscat. Examples may still be found in antique shops in the souks – commanding prices that would astound their original owners.

The introduction of rifles brought a new dimension to marksmanship, enabling tribesmen to pick off a gazelle – or an opponent – at hitherto unimaginable distances. Fortunately for those in the sights, as tribal wars became a thing of the past and the stocks of gazelle rapidly diminished, weapons became more a matter of decoration.

A young boy with his most prized possession.

Noor Ali's picture of these resting
gentlemen recalls, in an Arabian
version, Cartier-Bresson's 1938
photograph 'On the Banks of
the Marne'.

These young men, traditionally
garbed and armed, were to see a
period of change unprecedented in
the history of the emirate.

FOR CENTURIES THE mode of existence had remained almost unchanged. Skills had been handed down from father to son, so that families and tribes became identified with particular occupations. Some would be experts in the construction and maintenance of the *falaj* system, some would farm the palm groves, yet others would lead a nomadic existence in the sands, searching for grazing for their animals. The tempo and style of their lives must then have seemed as fixed and unalterable as the stars in their courses.

But for the children of Al Ain a new world was just around the corner. When Sheikh Zayed was a boy in the 1920s the only education available to him was that from the *mu'allim*, Koranic teacher. Exercise books and formal teaching of languages, mathematics, history or geography there were none and the young Zayed's early notebook was a camel's shoulder bone on which, after polishing, it was possible to write. It was not until the late 1950s that the first modern school opened in Al Ain, partially funded by Sheikh Zayed himself. Now the young of the city have access to comprehensive educational facilities that will take them from kindergarten to university.

'On the job training': fathers would introduce their sons to their trade from a very early age.

This young girl is visibly intrigued by Noor Ali's camera.

VISIONS
OF CHANGE

Sheikh Zayed with Sheikh Mohammed
bin Khalifa and his son, Sheikh
Hamdan bin Mohammed.

Previous pages: Members of the
Abu Dhabi Defence Force stand
guard at the Maqta checkpoint.

WHEN SHEIKH ZAYED became the Ruler of Abu Dhabi, on 6 August, 1966 he provided vitally needed leadership. In its recent past, Abu Dhabi had been plagued with economic hardship and then a failure to use its oil income.

In the early part of the 20th century Abu Dhabi had suffered a period of instability as a result of divisions in the ruling family. Progress and development were virtually non-existent and the people's distress was further compounded by the decline in the pearl trade as a result of the Great War. Even by the frugal standards of normal life these were hard times indeed, with food shortages common.

It was not until 1928, when Sheikh Zayed's eldest brother, Sheikh Shakhbut, assumed power that there seemed to be any chance for improvement – but such hopes proved short-lived. Whilst pearling had enjoyed a modest recovery during the 1920s, the invention of the cultured variety in the following decade led to the immediate collapse of the price for natural pearls; and although an oil concession agreement had been signed in 1939, exploration – which would have resulted in additional payments – was not undertaken because of the Second World War.

However, in the mid-1950s hopes for better times were renewed by positive indications that there was oil in the emirate. By the beginning of the 1960s revenue from oil was beginning to flow into the nation's coffers. The problem that then confronted the people of Abu Dhabi was that it was not spent on development.

Sheikh Zayed is often seen seeking the advice of elders, as here with Ma'n bin Mohammed Al Dhahiri around 1965. It was during his years as the Ruler's Representative in Eastern Region that his leadership qualities were revealed.

Sheikh Zayed leaves the Al Husn Fort with his entourage. It was not an unfamiliar sight to see him discard his car and choose to proceed on foot instead.

BY 1966 SHEIKH Zayed was already an experienced leader. His natural abilities and the political experience he gleaned as his brother the Ruler's Representative in the Eastern Region since 1946 stood him in good stead when he was called to take the ultimate responsibility of ruling the emirate.

As early as the 1950s his abilities were tested as a territorial dispute arose with Saudi Arabia, which claimed ownership of Buraimi and two other Omani villages close to Al Ain. This problem was eventually removed as a result of a swift police action in 1955 by the British-officered Trucial Oman Scouts, acting with Sheikh Zayed's support.

Among reforms introduced by Sheikh Zayed during the 1950s was a complete re-structuring of the rules by which farmers were permitted to draw water from the *falaj* system. Repairing any *falaj* that needed it, he also built a new one, increasing the water supply to the oasis. Traditional agriculture benefited, as did the rest of the local economy.

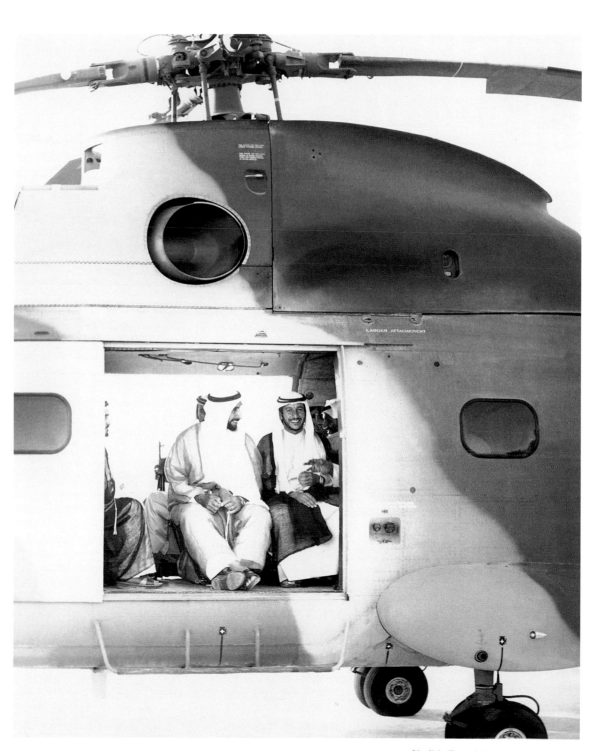

Sheikh Zayed frequently tours the emirate to review the progress of the projects he has initiated. Here, he used an Army helicopter, accompanied by adviser Hamouda bin Ali.

NOOR ALI HAS accompanied Sheikh Zayed on many of his foreign visits. He has always been impressed by his keen interest in the respective countries' infrastructures and development programmes, from the construction of hospitals and educational institutions to traffic systems. From these he would glean a wealth of advice and knowledge to take back to his own people. This way he ensured the very best quality and facilities for Abu Dhabi.

Noor Ali also noticed how attentive Sheikh Zayed was to innovative environmental opportunities ever since he became Ruler's Representative in the Eastern region. Indeed, he began planting ornamental trees along the dusty streets, and today, those trees and many thousands more have made Al Ain the greenest city in south-eastern Arabia.

In return for the friendship he has received from around the world, Sheikh Zayed subsequently helped settle disputes and bring about reconciliation through international mediation. Equally, he generously contributed to Third World education and welfare, empathising with the needs of less advanced communities, at a time when a bright future was dawning on Abu Dhabi.

A relaxed pose of Sheikh Zayed.

Margaret Mackay, a British parliamentarian and staunch supporter of Arab causes, meets Sheikh Zayed during his official visit to Britain in 1969. She lived in Abu Dhabi for a quarter of a century, dying there in 1996. Standing behind them is Noor Ali.

Sheikh Zayed and Sheikh Khalid with British diplomat, Edward Henderson.

DURING THE RULE of Sheikh Shakhbut the administration of the emirate had come to a near standstill, with decisions, when made, taking months to be reached. It was therefore one of Shéikh Zayed's first priorities on his succession to create an administrative structure which would enable the emirate to move into the modern age. As is customary in the Gulf, other family members were invited to share the responsibility. Sheikh Zayed chaired the Department of Finance and appointed his brother, Sheikh Khalid bin Sultan as Deputy Ruler. Sheikh Mohammed bin Khalid took the dual roles of Chairman of the Customs Department and Deputy Chairman of the Department of Finance. Sheikh Hamdan bin Mohammed was appointed to chair the departments of Public Works, Water Supply, Health, Education, Development, Telecommunications, and Civil Aviation – a multiplicity of responsibilities that would have daunted a lesser man. Sheikh Mubarak bin Mohammed took on the position of Chief of Police and Public Security, Sheikh Saif bin Mohammed became Chairman of Municipalities and Land Registration, Sheikh Surour bin Mohammed was appointed Chairman of the Department of Justice and Sheikh Khalifa bin Mohammed took responsibility for the Electricity Department. Sheikh Zayed's son, Sheikh Khalifa, succeeded his father as Ruler's Representative and Chairman of the Courts in the Eastern Region, while Sheikh Tahnoun bin Mohammed was appointed Mayor of Al Ain and Chairman of the Agriculture Department.

A Ruler at work. Sheikh Zayed discusses a point with his secretary Ahmed Obaidli.

Sheikh Zayed shares a lighter moment with the press.

Entering Al Husn Fort with, left,
Sheikh Hamdan bin Mohammed and,
right, Crown Prince Sheikh Khalifa.

Sheikh Zayed and Sheikh
Mohammed bin Khalifa with
Sheikh Mohammed bin Butti
outside the old fort.

Sheikh Zayed with Colonel Wilson,
then Commander of the Abu Dhabi
Defence Force.

MANY OTHER CITIZENS were encouraged to take up positions of responsibility in the rapidly developing emirate. Outside the Al Nahyan family, Sheikh Ahmed bin Hamed was appointed to run the Department of Labour, Sheikh Mohammed bin Butti became Ruler's Representative in Tarif, Sheikh Sultan bin Surour Al Dhahiri in Jebel Dhanna and Mubarak bin Hadhr on Das. Ahmed Khalifa Al Suweidi became the Ruler's Secretary and Adviser.

Whilst the Planning Council was headed by Sheikh Zayed, members of several prominent families also served – including Ahmed Khalifa Al Suweidi, Khalid Al Yousef and Mahmoud Hassan Juma. And, as the economy improved, people from Abu Dhabi who had been forced to leave in order to find work started to return, bringing with them valuable skills and experience.

The people wait to greet their Ruler at the gates of Al Husn Fort.

**Sheikh Zayed during the first
Accession Day celebrations.**

ONE OF MANY areas to receive Sheikh Zayed's attention in the late 1960s was the defence of the emirate. A decade earlier, in the mid-1950s, the British-officered Trucial Oman Scouts (TOS) had been sufficient to deal with problems arising out of the Saudi claim to the Omani part of Buraimi, but the development of Abu Dhabi's oil industry – and later the impending British withdrawal – compelled the emirate to build a defence capability of its own.

The Abu Dhabi Defence Force (ADDF) was established at the end of 1965, drawing upon the traditional military levies that had protected the Ruler and supplemented by officers seconded from the TOS. Following Sheikh Zayed's accession, plans were made to expand the force and within a couple of years its strength had grown to over 1,500 men, including officers seconded from Britain and from other Arab countries. It included a squadron of scout cars, a mortar corps, signals and transport units and a squadron that provided the Emiri Guard. In 1968, with the purchase of three inshore patrol craft, a Naval Wing was established and an Air Wing followed shortly after.

Land Rovers of the Abu Dhabi Defence Force pass the reviewing stand.

Ferret scout car driving past the crowds at an Accession Day parade.

THE ABU DHABI Defence Force, in common with military units around the world, were delighted to be able to take part in ceremonial occasions and played an important role in helping to forge a sense of national identity. In the years after Sheikh Zayed came to power his Accession Day was marked with a delightful mix of formal parades, sports events and casual mingling of the Ruler with his people – very different from the more structured occasions of today, when a bouquet from an airline stewardess would have little chance of being personally delivered!

A British Overseas Airways Corporation hostess presents the Ruler with a bouquet.

A decorative arch erected by the United Bank.

Sheikh Zayed congratulates Sheikh
Hamad bin Hamdan who rode the
winning horse in one
of the Accession Day races.

TO MODERN EYES, more accustomed to the terrible weapons of the 1990s, the equipment pictured here looks almost benign. Nonetheless, by the local standards of the time, the ADDF was a powerful force, and its regular desert exercises were attended not only by Sheikh Zayed but also by visiting heads of state and ministers from neighbouring countries. Few would then have foreseen the conflict that would involve the countries of the Gulf in the liberation of Kuwait just a generation later.

Ferret scout cars of the Abu Dhabi Defence Force on exercises near Al Ain in around 1970, keenly watched by ADDF personnel.

Sheikh Zayed, centre, with Sheikh Rashid of Dubai, left, and Sheikh Hamad bin Isa Al Khalifa, Crown Prince of Bahrain follow exercises.

A signals unit keeps in touch with the exercises.

THE TRUCIAL OMAN Levies were formed in 1951, becoming the Trucial Oman Scouts in 1956. Sheikh Zayed, foreseeing the benefits of the force, encouraged the Bedouin to enlist, and people from Abu Dhabi formed an important part of the corps. The Scouts later became the Union Defence Force, although both Abu Dhabi and Dubai maintained independent forces for some while after federation.

Neither a visitor from the American Wild West nor a bank robber – merely a visiting dignitary finding the blown sand something of a nuisance. How much more convenient, and elegant, is the keffiyeh!

Sheikh Zayed and the Crown Prince of Bahrain, testing light machine-guns.

C Squadron of the Trucial Oman
Scouts kept their headquarters at
Al Ain spick and span.

THE DISCOVERY OF oil, and its commercial exploitation, changed for ever the course of history for Abu Dhabi. In some parts of the emirate, as for example in Das, it was also to change the landscape.

Das, until its development in the 1960s, was a waterless, flat, rocky island, uninhabited by man and home only to thousands of pairs of terns during the breeding season. Too far offshore even to be of use to pearlers, Das – apart from the occasional visit by fishermen – was left to bake peacefully in the sun.

And then came the age of oil. On behalf of the concessionaires, Abu Dhabi Marine Areas (ADMA), an intensive survey began in 1953, much of it carried out by the renowned underwater explorer Commander Jacques Cousteau aboard his ship the Calypso. By May 1956, a promising structure had been identified around 30 kilometres from Das, and it was decided to drill ADMA's first exploration well.

New housing complexes were built – Camp Tell (Hill) for senior staff; Camp Wadi (Valley) for technical and clerical staff; and Camp Sahil (Plain) for labourers.

Crude oil was piped from the Umm Shaif field to Das for loading on to the tankers.

All equipment had to be brought in by air or sea from Bahrain.

IN JANUARY 1958 the drilling barge ADMA Enterprise began work and struck oil – in what was to become the giant Umm Shaif field – at the first attempt. Das was the obvious choice for the supply base and a harbour and airstrip were built, followed by housing, offices, a hospital and stores. Work began in 1960 on building a pipeline from the field to Das, and to install the facilities necessary for the bulk export of crude oil. In July 1962 BP's tanker British Signal, loaded with the first consignment of Umm Shaif crude, steamed off through the summer haze and into the history books.

These pictures, taken around 1962, show the early stages of construction of the terminal.

Mubarak bin Hadhr was appointed to be the Ruler's Representative on Das.

The flares indicate that the pipeline
had reached the island, but it
would seem that the storage
tanks had yet to be completed.

BUILDING A MODERN EMIRATE

Al Husn Fort in Abu Dhabi, as it was circa 1962. Home to the emirate's rulers from its construction in 1795 it now houses the Centre for Documentation and Research and The Cultural Foundation.

Previous pages: Al Husn Fort in the 1960s. As Abu Dhabi grew, so did its fort. The outer, square structure was added by Sheikh Shakhbut.

THE NAMELESS SANDY island bordering the southern shore of the Gulf was just one of many. Occasionally visited by pearlers and fishermen, sometimes wrecked by storms, it had otherwise remained pretty much undisturbed. Then, in 1761, a group of hunters of the Bani Yas tribe, straying far from their oasis home in Liwa, found a gazelle drinking at a fresh-water spring. They named the island Abu Dhabi – Homeland or Possession of the Gazelle. Some 30 years later Sheikh Shakhbut bin Dhiyab, the great-great-grandfather of Sheikh Zayed, built Al Husn Fort on the island which, much enlarged, still survives today. Now surrounded by the high-rise buildings of the modern city, it once stood alone save for a scattering of palm and *ghaf* trees and a few *barasti* huts.

Whilst the slender minarets of mosques now regularly pierce the skyline, just 30 years ago there were few.

Al Husn Fort: The tower on the left is known as the Eagle Tower, so called because an eagle made its nest there for many years, becoming stout on the tasty food given to it by the guards. The low, arched structure below the tower – containing a majlis, dining room and offices – was added in the 1960s by Sheikh Shakhbut when he started to use Al Husn as the seat of government.

IN STRONG CONTRAST to the years of inertia under Sheikh Shakhbut, on his accession in 1966 Sheikh Zayed immediately instituted his long-considered programme for the development of the infrastructure of the emirate. The Al Husn Fort became a centre of activity as town planners were recruited, architects briefed, contractors hired and equipment bought. Plans for roads, ports, bridges, airports, residential and office accommodation, hospitals, schools, water and sewerage systems, power generation and distribution were drawn up, considered and implemented in a frenzy of new construction projects.

At that time Abu Dhabi had no port, requiring ships to anchor offshore and discharge their cargoes into lighters – a slow, inefficient and sometimes hazardous method of handling, especially since everything from cement to food, cars to construction machinery had to be imported. But despite the difficulties the materials poured in and the transformation from obscure fishing village to modern metropolis commenced. So great was the need for development after so long a period of stagnation that, despite the burgeoning oil revenues, there were times when Abu Dhabi was actually spending more than it was earning.

Before the building of the port, everything had to be landed on the beach.

Soon after Sheikh Zayed became Ruler in 1966, he announced a number of major construction projects that would change the face of Abu Dhabi. Tons of steel, cement and other building materials were imported for this very purpose – as seen here lining the Corniche, from where they were distributed between specific projects.

The old Customs House on the Abu Dhabi Corniche, somewhere near today's Clock Tower.

Abu Dhabi's first high-rises – tiny beside some of today's buildings – were known as the threepenny bits, after the similarly shaped British coin.

IT MUST HAVE been a strange but exciting time to have lived in the city. In one area there would still be *barasti* huts amongst the *ghaf* trees, whilst in another, just a few hundred metres away, were rising new apartment blocks, complete with water, electricity, sewage disposal and what had to be considered as the ultimate luxury: air-conditioning.

Sheikh Zayed's determination that all citizens should share in the new-found wealth took a variety of forms. Occupants of the *barasti* huts were paid compensation when they were moved to make way for new development; citizens were given plots of land; foreign companies were required to find a local sponsor or partner. In these ways money was injected into the economy, whilst providing an environment that both encouraged and offered some protection to local entrepreneurs – most of whom at the time had little or no experience of trade or commerce.

The traffic police, smart in their white sleeves, arrived before the roads and, indeed, before most vehicles.

A nation in transition – the old and the
new meet in front of the Eastern Bank.

Foundations of the Maqta bridge under construction.

THE ISLAND OF Abu Dhabi is separated from the mainland by a shallow channel – a defensive advantage in the more unsettled times of the past, but also an obstruction to trade and transport. At Maqta, meaning 'crossing point', people, camels and vehicles could ford the stream only at low tide.

In the early 1950s, Petroleum Development (Trucial Coast), later to become the Abu Dhabi Petroleum Company (ADPC), paid for a narrow causeway to be built across the straight. Costing 1,000 pounds sterling, it served as the only access for vehicles from 1952 to 1968.

Upon his accession as Ruler of Abu Dhabi, Sheikh Zayed moved rapidly to improve communications between the capital and the rest of the emirate. One of his first decisions was to order the construction of a bridge to replace the causeway, and to dredge the channel around the back of the island to permit its use at all stages of the tide. Designed by consultants Cansult, the bridge and its approach roads were completed in 1968, when the old causeway was demolished.

Previous pages: Crossing the causeway to Abu Dhabi island before the Maqta bridge was built.

The main span of the bridge begins
to take shape.

THE MAQTA BRIDGE revolutionised contacts between Abu Dhabi and the mainland but, in a sign of the changing times, it cost 1,000 times more than the causeway, a total of one million pounds sterling.

As modern-day motorists whizz across the bridge they may notice a small watch-tower built in the middle of the channel to protect access to the island. Now restored (and, at night, basking in the glow of municipal floodlights) it provides a telling echo of distant days when, in 1856, it played a central role in the last battle to take place on Abu Dhabi island.

An aerial view of the Maqta bridge soon after its completion, looking east.

Anyone setting foot on the island had to report to the checkpoint, to obtain permission to proceed.

The Maqta bridge complete, with the old checkpoint on the right-hand side.

Modern Al Ain is beginning to take shape, as are some of its main arteries and, on the left, the Clock Tower roundabout.

BY FOOT OR on camel, stopping at the few scattered wells that lay along the route, people have been making the arduous 160-kilometre journey across the desert between the inland oasis of Al Ain and the coast near Abu Dhabi for thousands of years. Even as late as 1902 the then British Political Agent in Muscat, Major (later Sir) Percy Cox, recorded that it took him four hours to get from Abu Dhabi to the Maqta crossing and a further 37 hours to reach Al Ain.

Thus it remained for another half century, until the first motor vehicles came into use in the emirate – although even then it stayed a tortuous and hard trek. Those early four-wheel-drive vehicles and tough Bedford trucks would frequently become stuck and have to be dug out, and the journey could last from late afternoon through the night until the middle of the next day.

Preparing the ground – at first sight these machines must have intrigued many a camel.

Rolling tar on top of an embankment that lifted the road above the treacherous salt flats.

Another construction site in the desert not far from Al Ain. The ready availability of sweet sand was a great help in preparing the concrete for the road's foundations.

THROUGHOUT THE 1950s and early '60s traffic between Al Ain and Abu Dhabi continued to increase, largely because of the growth of Al Ain itself under the governance of Sheikh Zayed. Keen to move ahead with development and stimulate commerce, he urged his brother Sheikh Shakhbut to build a simple, hard-packed track across the desert. But Shakhbut, ever cautious of innovation, refused.

When Sheikh Zayed came to power, he gave a British consortium the task of planning the highway. A sum of 12.5 million Bahraini dinars (9.5 million pounds sterling) was set aside for the construction of what has now become one of the emirate's most essential lifelines. And, to the amazement of many, down the centre of the new dual carriageway were planted trees and oleander bushes, the first harbingers of a programme of planting that has transformed this desert land.

Roads were also upgraded within
the city of Al Ain.

Fields irrigated by a falaj on the outskirts of Al Ain.

WHILST DEVELOPMENT IN the capital progressed rapidly, inland the pace of change was a little slower. In the oasis of Al Ain the traditional methods of agriculture continued as they had for generations, thanks to the *falaj* system which made the growing of crops possible. And in the desert itself the nomadic lifestyle of the Bedouin and their herds of goats and sheep endured largely unaffected by the momentous events taking place elsewhere in the emirate.

One of the greatest problems which had always faced the people of Abu Dhabi was access to adequate supplies of fresh water – the occasional wells in the desert and along the coast being erratic and often brackish. But now oil revenues provided the money to search for new sources as well as transport water over long distances.

Water channels like these have supplied the needs of Al Ain since the Iron Age.

Amidst all the changes that were taking place these Bedouin shepherds maintained their traditional way of life.

77

**Drilling for water on the edge of
the desert.**

ABU DHABI'S FIRST guaranteed water
supplies, before the commissioning of
desalination plants, were provided by the
20th century equivalent of a *falaj* – a
pipeline that snaked across the desert from
Al Ain to the capital. There was even
enough left to irrigate the newly
established parks and gardens that were
softening the landscape of the emirate.
Even in these early days Sheikh Zayed was
implementing his vision of changing the
face of the emirate with a programme of
planting – not only the aesthetically
appealing trees and flowers in ornamental
gardens and along roads, but also the
more practical development of fruit and
crop farming.

An ornamental garden takes shape
in Al Ain.

ALTHOUGH SHEIKH SHAKHBUT had agreed, somewhat reluctantly, to allow Britain's Imperial Airways to establish an emergency landing strip at Abu Dhabi as long ago as 1934, it was not until after the Second World War that aviation made any real progress in the emirate. The first visitors were the oil companies which, in the 1950s, constructed an airfield just a few kilometres out of town by grading and rolling a conveniently flat piece of desert. Here, later, the DC-3s of Gulf Aviation would land, their Pratt and Whitney Twin Wasp engines growling in the hot desert air. Amongst Sheikh Zayed's priorities was the building of an airport of international standards at Bateen, which opened in 1968. Such was the pace of progress that a mere 14 years later it was superseded by a new, larger airport.

Sheikh Zayed departing on one of his many visits to neighbouring countries.

Das Island's airstrip. It is the search for oil which gave modern aviation in the Gulf its foundations.

Abu Dhabi Airport, late 70s.

THE QUEST
FOR UNITY

A meeting of the Trucial States Development Council in the mid-60s, under the chairmanship of the Ruler of Ras Al Khaimah.

Previous pages: 2 December, 1971; the flag of the newly formed United Arab Emirates flies for the first time.

AT THE BEGINNING of 1968, after nearly 150 years in the Gulf, the British informed the leaders of the Trucial States that they would be withdrawing from the region in 1971. So, in the midst of trying to transform his own state, Sheikh Zayed was also faced with the task of planning how Abu Dhabi and its fellow emirates might combine to form a nation that would not merely survive but prosper. On 18 February, 1968 Sheikh Zayed and Sheikh Rashid bin Saeed Al Maktoum of Dubai met at the tiny settlement of As Sameeh on the border of the two emirates. Together they established the basis of the federation, a union which they invited the Rulers of the other emirates – as well as those of Qatar and Bahrain – to join. Eventually Qatar and Bahrain decided on independence outside the federation, but the Rulers of the Trucial States agreed in 1971 to establish the UAE.

Sheikh Zayed welcomes Sheikh Isa, Ruler of Bahrain, on the eve of a round of federation talks.

**The Rulers of the Trucial States and of Qatar and Bahrain
after a meeting to discuss the formation
of a federation of nine emirates.**

A break for lunch: Sheikh Zayed,
Sheikh Khalid of Sharjah and Sheikh
Mohammed of Fujairah.

AT A MEETING held in Dubai on 25 February, 1968 – just seven days after the historic agreement reached by Sheikh Zayed and Sheikh Rashid at As Sameeh – the Rulers of the seven emirates together with those of Bahrain and Qatar agreed to work together with a view to forming a federation. A Supreme Council was established, made up of the Rulers of the nine states, which set about the difficult task of drawing up a charter for the federation and formulating mutually agreeable policies. Throughout 1969 and 1970 the Council met regularly, but it became apparent that it would not be possible to reach an agreement that would encompass the requirements of all parties. The Deputy Rulers then attempted to redraft the provisional constitution in a way that would accommodate the differing points of view – but despite these efforts Bahrain and Qatar eventually decided to establish separate independent states.

Despite this apparent setback, Sheikh Zayed and Sheikh Rashid pursued the quest for unity with the other five emirates that would eventually comprise the UAE. At a summit of the Rulers held in Dubai on 18 July, 1971, the original constitution was accepted as the provisional basis for the new country, which it was agreed would come into existence on 2 December, 1971. Ras Al Khaimah, whilst welcoming the formation of the UAE, had reservations over some aspects regarding representation – but on 10 February, 1972 it too elected to join the new country.

Sheikh Zayed, Sheikh Rashid bin Humaid – Ruler of Ajman, and British Political Agent Julian Bullard.

Sheikh Zayed gathered with other Rulers and dignitaries after a federation meeting. It is at these meetings that the new state and the new government progressively took shape.

The country's leaders, 1973. From left: Sheikh Rashid bin Ahmed Al Mualla, Crown Prince of Umm Al Quwain; Sheikh Sultan bin Mohammed Al Qassimi, Ruler of Sharjah; Sheikh Rashid bin Saeed Al Maktoum, Vice-President and Prime Minister of the UAE and Ruler of Dubai; Sheikh Zayed bin Sultan Al Nahyan, President and Ruler of Abu Dhabi; Sheikh Saqr bin Mohammed Al Qassimi, Ruler of Ras Al Khaimah; Sheikh Mohammed bin Hamad Al Sharqi, Ruler of Fujairah; Sheikh Humaid bin Rashid Al Nuaimi, Crown Prince of Ajman.

THE YEARS OF planning and negotiation were brought to a successful conclusion on 2 December, 1971 when the Rulers of the individual sheikhdoms formed the United Arab Emirates by the signing of the provisional constitution. The constitution, rather than attempting immediately to bind the different emirates into a rigid and uniform federation, provided a framework within which the various component parts of the new country could gradually adapt to the revised circumstances without the need for sudden, disruptive change. The old, respected systems of administration, individual to each emirate, could then be adapted to the federal needs over a period of time, allowing continuity and a smooth transition from the traditional to the new.

Under the constitution of the UAE, responsibility for general policy decisions lies with the Supreme Council of Rulers. The Council of Ministers – headed by the Prime Minister and accountable to the Supreme Council – has executive authority. The Cabinet, in which each emirate is represented, is responsible for the initiation of legislation. The Federal National Council – whose members are appointed by the Rulers – supervises and controls the implementation of projects.

A quarter of a century on, the effectiveness of the system agreed by Sheikh Zayed and Sheikh Rashid – back in the very different world of 1968 – has been amply proven. They had seen the future – and it worked.

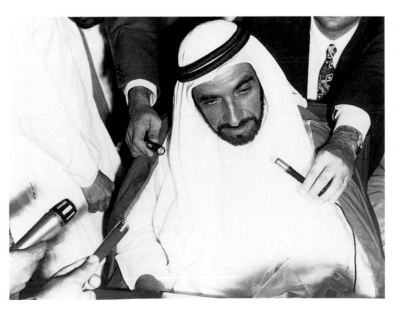

Announcement of the Federation by Sheikh Zayed on 2 December, 1971.

2 December, 1971 – the raised flag was then symbolic of the dramatic scale to which the country would reach in the future.

Sheikh Zayed addressing the Cabinet.

DURING THE CRUCIAL years leading to and immediately following the federation, Sheikh Zayed's responsibilities were two-fold. Besides leading the discussions for the formation of the country, he also needed to consolidate the government of the Abu Dhabi emirate.

Sheikh Zayed's plans for the rapid development of Abu Dhabi brought both power and responsibility to a new generation of leaders. The old system that combined, extraordinarily, absolute rule on the one hand with a patriarchal near-democracy on the other had been in place for at least 2,000 years, and had worked well in the less complex environment of the pre-oil era. Sheikhs ruled by the principle of 'first amongst equals', and maintained their positions by virtue of their accomplishments. It was not unusual, when a ruler lost support, for a self-correcting mechanism to come into play and for a more able leader to be acknowledged by the population.

Members of the Federal National Council during their first session.

Sheikh Mubarak Al Nahyan, Sheikh
Tahnoun, Sheikh Saif and Sheikh
Surour: four brothers who all took
on government responsibilities.

Sheikh Mubarak, the country's first Minister of the Interior.

TO ACHIEVE THE successful, seamless evolution from the old mechanism of governance to the more intricate and demanding requirements of a modern state required consultation and consensus. And, as the weeks and months passed after Sheikh Zayed's accession, a working and effective team of modern leaders took their places in the newly created ministries. Many also became federal ministers in 1971.

Whilst now, in the closing years of the century, inter-emirate co-operation is taken for granted, the building of a united nation from such disparate and fiercely independent components was then viewed by many as being, at least, optimistic. The task was undoubtedly made easier by the solid experience gained through the establishment of the administrative system in Abu Dhabi – providing a model on which the federal system could be based.

Former Foreign Minister Ahmed bin Khalifa Al Suwaidi, now adviser to the President, with his son Mohammed.

Sheikh Sultan bin Surour Al Dhahiri,
the Ruler's Representative at Jebel
Dhanna with a member of
the Abu Dhabi Defence Force.

THE FORMATION – AND successful subsequent development – of the federation depended then, as to some extent it still does, on a strong partnership between the emirates, achieved through goodwill and mutual understanding between the Rulers. Whilst all contributed enormously, nowhere were the bonds closer than between Sheikh Zayed and Sheikh Rashid.

Meetings were frequent as the Rulers set about the task of creating the federation, establishing common policies in such diverse matters as foreign affairs, defence, immigration, social services and security.

Sheikh Zayed and Sheikh Rashid share halwa during a pause between sessions. Their respect for one another enabled them to overcome the obstacles to the federation.

Previous pages: Sheikh Zayed and Sheikh Rashid.

Sheikh Zayed, Sheikh Saqr, Ruler of Ras Al Khaimah, and Sheikh Maktoum, then Crown Prince of Dubai, at Accession Day celebrations.

A gathering of Rulers and leading
personalities. Seen here are Sheikh
Zayed, Sheikh Khalid of Sharjah,
Sheikh Mohammed of Fujairah and
Sheikh Saqr of Ras Al Khaimah.

King Hussein of Jordan receives a warm welcome.

Saab Salam of Lebanon inspects a guard of honour at Abu Dhabi Airport.

AFTER DECADES OF isolation, Abu Dhabi was beginning to emerge from obscurity and to make its presence felt on the world stage. As oil revenues started to come in, the emirate rapidly acquired a reputation for supporting worthy organisations, and indeed countries, with donations. Even before the formation of the UAE, Abu Dhabi contributed substantial funds to the Trucial States Development Council and in 1972 the Abu Dhabi Fund for Arab Economic Development was established, with a capital of $500 million. Other acts of generosity in the early part of the decade included a grant of $20 million for the Arab-African Development Bank, another for $60 million for the construction of the Suez pipeline and a contribution of $33 million towards the re-opening of the Suez Canal.

Abu Dhabi has since, as a member of the UAE, played a leading role in the Gulf Co-operation Council, Arab League, Islamic Conference Organisation and OPEC.

From 1967 onwards the emirate was visited by numerous heads of state and other dignitaries, from both the Arab world and nations further afield.

**Sultan Qaboos of Oman, left, with
Sheikh Mubarak in Al Ain in 1973.**

RETAINING TRADITIONAL VALUES

Sheikh Zayed and his eldest son Sheikh Khalifa bin Zayed, Crown Prince of Abu Dhabi.

SHEIKH ZAYED HAS always been very much a family man and has promoted and encouraged the maintenance of traditional family values amongst his people – particularly important during a period of rapid change probably unequalled by any other country.

Naturally the education of his own sons has been one of his prime concerns. From an early age they had been encouraged to recognise and prepare for the roles they would one day play in the governance of the country. Whilst Sheikh Zayed's eldest son, Sheikh Khalifa, succeeded his father as Ruler's Representative in Al Ain in 1966 – and became Crown Prince in 1968 – his younger sons have also all taken up the responsibilities of state as they grew to manhood, as indeed have his grandsons. Other members of the Al Nahyan family – including Sheikh Zayed's cousins – have also been involved in government, with many of them holding senior positions in which they guided the country throughout the extraordinary changes and developments of the past 30 years.

Previous pages: Sheikh Zayed leads his cousins Sheikh Mubarak and Sheikh Tahnoun in a celebratory dance at a wedding.

Scouts on parade: from left, Sheikh Sultan bin Zayed, now Deputy Prime Minister; Sheikh Mohammed bin Zayed, Chief of Staff; Sheikh Hamdan bin Zayed, Minister of State for Foreign Affairs.

Beyond the political links, the Rulers and political figures of the various emirates also had very close relationships. It was not unusual to see them gathered together at weddings, traditional camel races and other sporting events. From left: Sheikh Mohammed bin Khalifa; Sheikh Zayed; Sheikh Rashid Al Nuaimi, late Ruler of Ajman and Sheikh Shakhbut.

Three generations: Sheikh Zayed
with his sons, Hamdan, Hazza and
Tahnoun and his grandson Sultan bin
Khalifa.

BEFORE FEDERATION THERE were few schools and education, such as it was, relied upon Koranic teachers. In 1969 just 9,000 students were registered for schools in Abu Dhabi. It was not until the early 1970s that the new federal government was able to make education free – and compulsory – to all. Many fathers and grandfathers – like Sheikh Zayed in the picture (right), would have taken a hand in the education of their children, imparting the history of the area and helping to maintain the traditional Arab values.

Help with homework – Sheikh Zayed
with his grandson Sultan bin
Khalifa, now Chairman of the
Crown Prince's Court.

Sheikh Zayed: A father figure to his
people's children.

FAMILIES, THEN AS now, gathering at Eid festivals, weddings and other occasions to celebrate together would perform traditional dances and music. The quick-thinking members of the family enjoyed the *Ijaza*, in which the participants would alternately recite rhyming lines of spontaneous verse – a mental exercise at which Sheikh Zayed excels.

Even the way names are constructed reinforce the family connections, combining the given name with that of the father and the tribe. Zayed bin Sultan Al Nahyan means Zayed, the son of Sultan, of the Al Nahyans.

From left: Sheikh Mansour bin Ahmed Al Thani, Sheikh Sultan bin Zayed, and Sheikh Mohammed bin Zayed, right, enjoy a joke at Sheikh Sultan's wedding.

Brothers Sheikh Khalifa and Sheikh Sultan.

Off-duty: Noor Ali's camera captures the
informal and playful side to the young elite,
during a wedding reception.

The community has always remained tightly knit around the principles of Islam.

THROUGHOUT ABU DHABI, in small villages or the capital itself, the physical affirmation of the Muslim faith is embodied in the mosques, where commoners and members of the ruling families, the wealthy and the less well-to-do, alike all worship together. Mosques, beautiful as so many of them are, are not merely for decoration: they attest to a religion that guides its adherents through every aspect of their lives and instils in Muslims a sense of community and mutual responsibility for each other. Islam asks every Muslim to respect every person, irrespective of his position in society – indeed *zakat*, the obligatory giving of alms to assist the less fortunate, is one of the five basic tenets of the religion.

Abu Dhabi's Grand Mosque.

Athletes from the Al Flash Sports Club.

Previous pages: Scouts of the Abu Dhabi Troop.

WHILST THE YOUTH of the emirate have been encouraged to maintain an interest in the traditional sports of hunting, falconry, camel racing, rowing and dhow sailing, other activities have also received official support. Sheikh Zayed's commitment to the development of all types of sporting activities – be they based on local sports or on imported pastimes from other parts of the world – is amply demonstrated in the comprehensive calendar of fixtures and the wide range of facilities now available, notably the spectacular Zayed Sports City stadium which hosts football matches and many other events.

But these facilities, in the late 1960s, were still a long way in the future. The simpler pleasures of scouting, athletics and school sports were then the standard, instilling in the young a sense of competition and personal discipline that were to serve the rising generation well in the years ahead. And what could be better than displaying one's prowess before one's Sheikh?

The sack race – sports were not always of an Olympic standard!

The flag of Abu Dhabi tops the
children's pyramid.

THE ARAB HORSE, small and agile, is justly famed throughout the world – indeed all racing thoroughbreds are descended from just three Arab horses introduced to Britain in the 18th century. Horses, although never in as common use as the camel in the UAE because their hooves are unsuited to soft sand, were still highly prized and in the 1920s Sheikh Zayed's family kept a stable of 180 – in addition to some 400 camels.

Early morning exercise for the men and horses of the Emiri Guard.

Sheikh Zayed inspecting a fine
Arab thoroughbred.

IN RECENT YEARS horse-racing has become a major sport in the calendar of the UAE – indeed the world's richest horse-race is held in the neighbouring emirate of Dubai. The UAE Equestrian Federation, based in Abu Dhabi, with Sheikh Sultan bin Khalifa Al Nahyan – Sheikh Zayed's grandson – as the chairman of its board, has done much to encourage the breeding of thoroughbreds in the UAE and co-ordinates the work of the country's equestrian clubs and their participation in both national and international events.

Sheikh Sultan bin Khalifa accompanying his horsemen before the start of a race during wedding festivities.

Sharing a love of horsemanship.

Nearing the finish.

ORIGINALLY A HUMBLE beast of burden, many camels are now bred exclusively for racing. The sport began as a method by which prospective buyers could test the strength and stamina of the animal, qualities that are demanded of today's beasts on race-tracks that can be up to 16 kilometres long. By tradition the jockeys are young boys whose light weight minimises the load.

In the 1960s the race-tracks were simple affairs set out on any convenient piece of desert, the course often being marked by an item that was becoming familiar in the region – the oil drum. Now meetings are held in more formal surroundings, with grandstands catering to the comfort of spectators.

The regular jostling at the start can
look quite alarming to a first-time
spectator of camel-racing.

SHEIKH ZAYED'S ABIDING interest in falconry, an ancient sport, commenced at an early age and by the mid-1920s he was already hunting with his own falcon. Probably invented in the rolling steppes of central Asia, falconry came to the Islamic world following the Muslim conquests which brought the Arabs into contact with the Byzantines and Persians. Yazid bin Muawiya, the Umayyad ruler from AD 680 to 683, was amongst the first recorded enthusiasts, setting a royal precedent that has continued in Arabia to the present day.

In the late 1940s a bird could be purchased for around US$30; by the 1960s that had risen to some $600. Both the *hurr* and the *shahin* falcons are favoured in the Gulf, although the *shahin* is generally accepted to be the better bird because of its high flight and extreme courage. The main prey in the emirates was the *houbara* or MacQueen's bustard (a powerful bird that can weigh up to four kilograms and stand as much as 75 centimetres tall) which can stun an attacker with its wing or squirt an unpleasant oily fluid into the falcon's eye, incapacitating it for days.

Arabs have remained keen falconers. The sport preserves their ties to the desert.

Falcons require intense training and conditioning before reaching peak performance.

Sheikh Zayed at ease with his falcon.

Oars at the ready... boat crew prepare for a traditional race.

THE PEOPLE OF Abu Dhabi have strong links with the sea. For generations the waters of the Gulf provided a route for trade, yielded food and, until the invention of the cultured pearl in the 1930s, provided a hard-won source of wealth.

Dhows are still built locally using materials and following designs that have changed little in centuries – except that nowadays the motive force is provided by powerful diesel engines rather than the wind. These sturdy vessels continue to ply between ports in the Gulf as well as making longer journeys to India, Pakistan and Africa. Sailing dhows, commonplace just a generation or so ago, are now usually built only for racing. These modern-day replicas of the dhows that were once used for fishing are about 12 metres in length. With their lateen-rigged sail attached to an 18-metre boom, they require enormous skill to sail.

Another popular traditional and competitive watersport is rowing. Up to as many as 200 chanting oarsmen power these heavy craft, their strokes kept in time by the rhythm of the drummer – perhaps the most enviable job on board.

Sheikh Zayed inspects a racing vessel under construction.

**Traditional boat races draw a keen
crowd of spectators.**

Drums are an essential accessory to the rhythmic choreography of traditional dances.

TRADITIONAL DANCE AND music: As in many societies around the world, music and dance form an important part of the cultural life of Abu Dhabi. Traditional instruments were simple, reflecting the limited materials available for their construction. Drums of various types were usually made of goatskin; goats' hooves were sewn on to a girdle and would rattle as the wearer danced; *tambouras* – something between a guitar and a harp – were made of wood and skin. Pipes, too, were not uncommon but were usually imported.

Traditional Bedu dance and song drew not only on Arabic and Islamic sources but also found inspiration in the music of Africa and the Indian sub-continent, with whom seafarers from the Gulf had long been trading. Pearl-divers developed a range of songs – one in particular, the *fjeri*, usually sung at the end of the day's work, being so loaded with the sadness of homesickness and distant loved ones that some still believe that the truly great exponents, called *nahams*, go blind with emotional and physical effort.

Previous pages: Everyone joins in the dance on festive occasions – here Abdul Jalil Al Fahim and Sheikh Saif bin Mohammed Al Nahyan lead the proceedings.

Regular groups of drummers would often travel quite a distance in order to perform their celebratory musical rituals at weddings and festivals.

THE PRESERVATION OF Abu Dhabi's heritage has always been of great importance to Sheikh Zayed, who believes that a "people who do not know their past can have no present and no future." Many citizens share his view – whilst all the benefits and advantages of a modern society are acknowledged they see no reason to abandon the traditional. Thus there has grown a pleasing sense of continuity that combines a general appreciation of the past with a sense of duty to the future.

During the years he spent in Al Ain and the surrounding mountains and desert Sheikh Zayed had been able to participate in the Bedouin way of life as well as that of the townsfolk and he is familiar with every aspect of his people's lives – from farming to hunting, camels to falconry, handicrafts to traditional dances.

The traditional dances may still be seen on festive occasions.

Women in their finery.

Overleaf: One of the most
spectacular traditional dances is
the naiashti in which colourfully
dressed girls swirl their hair to the
insistent rhythm of the music.

TRANSFORMATION

Pages 132-3: Apart from the familiar shape of Al Husn Fort it is hard to reconcile the Abu Dhabi of yesteryear with the sophisticated city of today.

Previous pages: By 1969 the outline of the new city was discernible.

By 1974 the future was taking shape. In the foreground the Sheikh Khalifa Mosque is under construction, whilst beyond the British Embassy compound rises the Mohammed bin Zayed Building – later to be dwarfed by the Baynunah Tower and Arab Monetary Fund Building.

THE TOWN PLANNERS had done their job well and in 1969 the grid pattern around which Abu Dhabi's development was to be based had begun to be transferred from blueprint to reality. By the end of this extraordinary decade the new city was taking shape, with work well under way on the construction of both the corniche and Port Zayed.

The central feature of the growing town remained the Al Husn Fort but other new landmarks were beginning to appear. The Grand Mosque was built and the main thoroughfare of Airport Road, now officially re-named Rashid bin Saeed Al Maktoum Street, stretched invitingly away inland towards the newly opened Maqta Bridge.

But at the turn of the decade Abu Dhabi still remained essentially a low-rise city, the tallest buildings being the two 'threepenny bits'. On the then outskirts of the town some of the areas that were to become parks still had their scattering of indigenous *ghaf* trees. And the glass-clad office blocks, towering hotels and multi-storey apartments of today's Abu Dhabi were yet in the future.

Despite the undeniable benefits of progress, parking would appear to have been easier 20 years ago.

**The modern city which has
earned the nickname
Manhattan of the Gulf.**

IT IS JUST 30 years since Sheikh Zayed's accession as Ruler of Abu Dhabi and the achievements of those three decades have probably never been equalled by any people anywhere around the globe. Whilst the transformation from tiny fishing village to modern city is remarkable enough, it is the pace of change that is astounding. What it took other countries centuries to accomplish through a slow process of evolution has been undertaken here in less than half a lifetime.

The Al Husn Fort which in 1969
stood isolated on the
sparsely-populated island,
is now dwarfed by high-rises.